A BOOK OF YOUR OWN

Also by Anne Dickson

A Woman in Your Own Right
The Mirror Within
Difficult Conversations
Reconnecting with the Heart
Teaching Men to be Feminist
Women on Menopause (with Nikki Henriques)
Hysterectomy (with Nikki Henriques)

A BOOK OF YOUR OWN

Inspirational Wisdom for Women,
Every Day of the Year

ANNE DICKSON

First published in the United Kingdom by Quartet Books,
a member of the Namara Group, in 1994

This edition published by Duckworth, in 2023

Duckworth, an imprint of Duckworth Books Ltd
1 Golden Court, Richmond, TW9 1EU, United Kingdom
www.duckworthbooks.co.uk

For bulk and special sales please contact
info@duckworthbooks.com

A CIP catalogue record for this book is available from the British Library

Text design and typesetting by Danny Lyle

Printed and bound in Great Britain by Clays Ltd, Elcograf S.p.A.

1 3 5 7 9 10 8 6 4 2

Paperback ISBN: 978-0-7156-5510-8
eISBN: 978-0-7156-5511-5

A BOOK OF YOUR OWN

JANUARY

1

The resolve to be a different and better person will soon evaporate; acceptance of yourself, as you are, is slower to cultivate but more steadfast.

2

It is curious how often we make the mistake of using our own behaviour as a central reference point when interpreting other people's behaviour.

3

Really good friends are those who interrupt your usual pattern with a reminder to be gentle on yourself and take the easier option.

4

People are usually quite happy to consider a clearly expressed request – it is the accumulated backlog of resentment that gets their backs up.

5

You can behave agreeably without having to pretend to agree.

6

When a female friend or colleague tries to be assertive and makes a mess of it, *that* is the moment she needs your support and congratulations for having taken the risk.

7

Pleasure and pride are incompatible with anxiety.

8

Taking the initiative instead of waiting for someone else to make the first move can be a seriously liberating experience.

9

Learn to distinguish between
what you can change
and what you can't.

10

Dependence on approval
is like any other addiction –
habit-forming and desperately
hard to overcome.

11

If you focus only on the absence of perfection, you can lose sight of the love contained in the present.

12

Regular periods of time for you to experience yourself alone are as vital to your emotional health as sleep.

13

Genuine acknowledgement of someone's anger can help defuse an explosive situation.

14

Our abiding need to please robs us of our personal power.

15

Care, given willingly, is free of charge; care, given grudgingly, stores up hidden costs.

16

Fear of success inhibits us more powerfully than fear of failure.

17

Rather than getting lost in 'what ifs' and 'if onlys', decide what you will settle for right now – and go for it.

18

Half-hearted or grudging participation in any sexual activity always stores up a measure of resentment.

19

Even the very young and the very old have the right to be considered as equals.

20

Imagine how you would look upon yourself if you had always been told that you were beautiful – then, for a day, behave 'as if'.

21

Be less mistrustful of your heart and more sceptical of the dictates of your head.

22

We try to be in control so much of the time that it is hard to allow others the freedom to have bad moods without feeling personally responsible.

23

However secretly you disapprove of someone, it will inevitably leak out in your communication with them.

24

Setting limits allows you to value your time and energy more highly.

25

If you trust something precious to someone else's care, you will be extremely careful who that person is: remember this when committing yourself to a lover.

26

Irritation at others' failure to live up to expectations often correlates to the way we punish ourselves when we fail to live up to our own.

27

A refusal with an open heart allows you to care and to say no at the same time.

28

When the whole situation makes you unhappy and confused, choose *one* thing, however small, that you would like to change.

29

When you look in the mirror first thing in the morning, interrupt the critical voices in your head by looking at your reflection and saying, 'Good morning, friend'.

30

Criticising others for being too dependent voices, indirectly, a desperate longing to be taken care of ourselves.

31

Finding your own voice is crucial – learn to breathe deeply, play with different sounds and don't worry about who might hear or what they might think.

FEBRUARY

1

Resentment that your needs have been ignored can be a sign that you have spent too long harbouring unspoken wishes instead of expressing them out loud.

2

It is extremely frustrating for others when we persistently avoid taking responsibility for making our own decisions.

3

If you wait until you *feel* assertive before you tackle a particular situation, you'll probably never do it.

4

Only robots can say no without feeling guilty.

5

Never allow yourself to be pressurised into making an instant decision – always give yourself permission to ask for time to think it over, whether you need an hour, a day or a week.

If we have no clear boundaries, we can experience no real freedom.

7

It is sometimes easier to find fault with those to whom you are closest than to express your appreciation of them.

8

Try to take responsibility for your refusal instead of portraying yourself as a helpless victim of other people or events.

9

It is assertive to know when to yield graciously to impossible odds.

10

True humility is only possible when your self-esteem is high.

11

It is never too late in life to awaken a dormant talent.

12

Remember you are still precious even when someone treats you like shit!

13

For most of us, put-downs are more effectively handled with honesty and clarity than with an attempt at wit.

14

Only conditional love is blind – genuine love allows us to see and love everything inclusively.

15

Acknowledging feelings of envy can show you where and how to set your own sights higher.

16

We often undermine our authority by indulging our need to be liked when it would be sufficient and more appropriate to settle for being respected.

17

The more you try to change someone, the more they will resist.

18

A life spent constantly restrained by the need for others' approval is a life spent in captivity.

19

It is the holding back of tears that is painful – not the release.

20

However hard we try to control everything that's happening, we *still* get taken by surprise.

21

Your own insight in your own time has the greatest meaning and value.

22

One way we can put ourselves down is by failing to ask for adequate financial compensation for the work we do.

23

Try and acknowledge your tiredness *before* you collapse – the longer you leave it, the harder it becomes to say 'enough'.

24

If you need to take time to consider a decision, say so clearly – don't allow yourself to be rushed to suit someone else's pace.

25

The pressure to always be pleasing in our behaviour and our appearance distorts our spirits in the same way that the ancient practice of foot binding distorted women's feet.

26

If it *really* didn't matter, you wouldn't be spending so much time thinking about it.

27

Love and anger are said to be incompatible bedfellows – but they certainly enjoy a passionate and lifelong love affair.

28

It is important to keep sight of your own beauty even when others fail to see it.

29

Sometimes the only way to leap is to close your eyes, surrender and trust.

MARCH

1

It's easy to get trapped between two narrow alternatives: either I'm to blame or you're to blame. In fact, some things just *happen*.

2

In reality, we are rarely held captive by the demands of others – more often we are held captive only by the limits of our imagination.

3

It is *really* too late?

4

Take the risk of asking
for a hug when you
feel in need of one.

5

Automatic apologies, however abject, are usually intended to deflect the other person's anger; they have little to do with genuine assumption of responsibility or sincere regret.

Just because you're in a minority of one, doesn't necessarily mean that you are wrong.

7

Making decisions inappropriately on behalf of others is a form of oppression.

8

You are worth respecting even when you don't get the respect you deserve.

9

When you want to ask for more money, start by stating the specific sum you have in mind instead of referring vaguely to an 'increase' and letting the other person guess.

10

Fear of isolation prevents you from being truly in touch with your personal power.

11

A spontaneous expression of gratitude is more valuable than a planned and polished performance.

12

If you're feeling anxious about an important conversation, face-to-face interaction is far more effective than digital communication.

13

The longer you wait to take an initiative, the greater the risk that your anxiety will get the better of you.

14

Try simply enjoying our differences – without the automatic labels of better or worse.

15

No one could make you *feel* insignificant if you weren't disposed to believe you were insignificant in the first place.

16

You don't have to strive to prove to others you are lovable – you are lovable just as you are.

17

Sing, dance, paint for the sheer pleasure of it – instead of getting lost in achieving marks for artistic performance!

18

An aggressive approach provokes an aggressive response.

19

Determination to have everything *now* can prevent us discovering all sorts of other options that lie in store for us if we can only take a deep breath . . . and wait!

20

If listening to a particular conversation is making you feel uncomfortable, you can choose to walk away from it.

21

It may only be a tiny grievance, but air it anyway.

22

Value those friends who help you laugh at yourself when you tend to become over-serious.

23

Opening your heart to the experience of love inevitably leaves your heart open to the experience of loss.

24

Nobody welcomes criticism.

25

Asking clearly and specifically lets the other person know *what* it is you want – this gives them a clear choice about how to respond.

26

A statement which begins with 'I feel that . . . ' is nothing to do with your feelings – it is usually a substitute for 'I think that . . . '.

27

If you keep waiting for the right moment to speak up, you'll find the moment has passed you by.

28

Playing the role of 'the martyr' in the present encourages the desire for rescue and reward in the future.

29

You can enjoy sexual attraction to someone without feeling compelled to *do* anything about it.

30

The first step in learning to express your emotions is to stop lying to yourself about what you really feel.

31

A little outrageousness never did anyone any harm.

APRIL

1

Simply because a clever put-down makes others laugh, doesn't stop it being hurtful to the recipient.

Confronting a situation when it slightly irritates you helps you handle it effectively and harmlessly. The longer you let the pressure build, the more likely you are to explode, with damaging and hurtful consequences.

2

3

Most women find fatigue very difficult to acknowledge, so instead of listening to our bodies, we often push them beyond healthy limits.

4

Instead of wasting emotional energy worrying about someone's opinion of you, ask them directly.

5

Isn't it extraordinary how easily we hand over our power on a plate and then get angry when someone helps themselves to it?

Your sexuality is a vital part of your being even if you're not currently sexually 'doing' anything.

7

Try not to turn down authentic care, when offered to you, even if it isn't packaged in exactly the way you had in mind.

8

If you begin by saying, 'Hello, I'm sorry . . .', you introduce yourself as an apology. You'll find it hard going trying to move from that starting point.

9

Even good advice, if excessive, will obstruct the capacity of the individual to think and decide for themself.

10

Accompanying your refusal with an explanation can be courteous. Offering elaborate excuses is usually an attempt to persuade the other person not to disapprove of you.

11

If you try to soothe away someone else's anger to lessen your own discomfort, you'll only make them angrier.

12

Remember that when you're down and tired, you're more likely to interpret every 'mishap' too personally.

13

If you make a vague, indifferent request, you are likely to get a vague, indifferent response.

14

It is always tempting to win – the price is a loss of equality.

15

Remind yourself you exist as you, apart from all your roles and responsibilities.

16

Does it really matter if people think you're crazy some of the time?

17

You can approach your life as a unique work of art or as an inherited template which you have to adhere to relentlessly.

18

Each time you say yes when you really want to say no, you mark up another notch of resentment.

19

Whatever fee you ask for will be too much in some people's eyes and too little in others'.

20

You don't have to stay and listen to someone who is talking at you – you can close the conversation and leave.

21

If you are certain of your *right* to a service you are paying for, you will be able to complain clearly, without putting anyone down.

22

When making a to-do list, add at least one pleasurable activity for yourself so that the importance of self-care doesn't slip your mind.

23

Someone in great distress sometimes just needs a caring and quiet presence – not analysis or advice.

24

No risk, or change, is ever too small to be significant.

25

It is easy to overreact and misinterpret online communication; be prepared to clarify instead of jumping to conclusions.

26

Care rooted in compassion is quite different from care rooted in compulsion: the former is given willingly, the latter is extracted through fear of censure or disapproval.

27

We cannot be held responsible for what we feel – only for how we choose to act on our feelings.

You can clearly state your profound disagreement with someone else's opinion and *still* leave them the right to believe what they want.

28

29

It may be just a tiny little thing – but it could well be an *important* tiny little thing.

30

In an assertive transaction, power is an ongoing part of the process and has little to do with who 'wins'.

MAY

1

The more you can allow others the freedom to express feelings of irritation and anger towards you, the less likely they are to stockpile resentment.

2

If a compliment gives you both embarrassment and pleasure, it is more rewarding for the other person if you express both these feelings honestly than if you try to disguise your embarrassment with a hastily contrived compliment of your own in return.

3

Start small – celebrate – and build from there.

4

When reflecting on the emotional cost of a relationship, it's always tempting to blame the other rather than acknowledge your own unclear or inadequate communication. Try to be honest about the past.

5

If you say no, looking at the person directly, without smiling and in a firm tone of voice, they'll know you mean it.

If you're always the one who gives in a relationship and never takes, it can never be equal. Tell your partner what *you* need.

7

Essentially, feelings are neither positive nor negative – this division is based on what is desirable or undesirable in any given culture.

8

Each time you acknowledge your anxiety and go ahead anyway, you strengthen your self-esteem, no matter the outcome.

9

The totally assertive woman exists only in our minds – she is not real!

10

Both irritation and pleasure are best expressed spontaneously.

11

It is difficult to overestimate the conflict we face when saying no because it flies in the face of all the accommodating behaviour we have ever learned.

12

However clear, direct and assertive a request may *sound*, it is always aggressive if it leaves the other person with no choice.

13

The lower our self-esteem, the greater our need to be right.

14

However deeply you're convinced that you know what is best for someone else, you still run the risk of a subtle emotional takeover.

15

We need to experience separateness as much as we need to experience closeness.

16

In real life, there is almost no adequate compensation for adopting the role of the martyr.

17

Releasing some of the stored-up feelings from your past helps you to be clearer about what you are feeling in the present.

18

However lovingly, thoughtfully and caringly, it is still possible to give people *too* much.

19

A steamroller, no matter how quietly and gently it moves, will still crush everything in its path.

20

It is hard to allow others to simply 'forget' things when we, ourselves, are trying so hard to remember everything for everybody.

21

Become familiar with your emotions – recognise them, experience them, learn not to be frightened of them.

22

It is easier to accept someone's disappointment in the short term when you know that your change of mind is more truthful for you in the long term.

23

If your suggestion is ignored, you can either sulk or make the suggestion again, adding clearly that you would welcome a response.

24

Learn which elements soothe and revitalise you – then make the time to be near water or fire, in the air or close to the earth.

25

Automatic self-reproach can mask a tendency to avoid feelings of anger.

26

Each time we say, 'I'm no good at . . . ', we suppress the possibility of the fun of learning.

27

If you are unable to express intimate feelings of anger and grief with a partner, you will find it difficult to express the vulnerability of sexual arousal.

28

It is so easy to underestimate the beauty and value of what we give to others.

29

It is impossible to be creative with your life *and* to worry about what people think of you – so the choice is which one to give up.

30

Put-downs are powerful – an unchallenged one can remain clear in the memory for years afterwards.

31

Remind yourself you're a passionate, hot-blooded woman even if no one currently fancies you.

JUNE

1

You don't need to understand *why* someone's crying to be supportive – just *be* there.

2

When you make a complaint, include a specific alternative so that the other person knows what you would prefer.

3

Our reactions to others are rooted in our own image of ourselves.

4

Giving sometimes offers us an easier, less risky option than daring to take.

5

If, when offering a criticism, you are really aiming for a total personality transformation, you'll find your words understandably rejected.

If you refuse to be strait-jacketed by other people's expectations, you'll find far more creative opportunities open to you.

7

When you've done the
brave and right thing but are
tormented by self-doubt,
contact a loving friend
and ask for reassurance.

8

As you summon up the courage
to confront a long-standing
source of irritation, take a
moment to consider your own
limits – what will you do if the
other person refuses to change?

9

If you find it hard to confront a put-down, it may be because deep down you are afraid it might be true.

10

Trying to reach an orgasm in the face of feeling resentful, tearful or depressed is a form of self-denial and self-punishment.

11

Sometimes the blanket feeling of rejection is only a thin covering for a much deeper sense of outrage.

12

Don't be afraid to give a compliment to someone on the grounds that you don't know the person well enough.

13

Listen attentively to what your body, in its wisdom, tells you.

14

If you ask for more money at work, don't be drawn into comparisons with your colleagues – keep the discussion centred on your own request and your own situation.

15

Trying to make your father or mother into the parent you would have preferred is a waste of energy.

16

Taking the time to explore and release stored-up emotions can greatly enhance your self-esteem.

17

When you catch yourself thinking, 'If only . . . ', you'll find your eyes are closed to the creative opportunities of the present.

18

The cloying sweetness of approval spoils our taste for personal power.

19

Suppressing our feelings of hurt inevitably suppresses our feelings of joy.

If you have something important to say, always wait until you have the other person's full attention before starting to speak.

20

21

Learning to rid yourself of a negative self-image is like undoing a Russian doll – you keep thinking you've got to the core of it and then you find there's still another layer.

22

Pleading powerlessness is sometimes a more comfortable option than acknowledging choice.

23

Remember you have a right to privacy – don't allow yourself to be pressurised into answering questions which feel intrusive.

24

Capping one put-down with another 'better' one enhances the use of aggression as an emotional weapon.

25

The problem with frequently putting yourself down is that it makes it difficult for anyone to get near enough to offer even a small honest criticism of their own.

26

Investing too much effort into being caring and considerate ourselves can make us furious with others who choose not to live up to our excessively high standards.

27

The more deeply you reject yourself, the more fearful you become of being rejected by others.

28

Go ahead and be ridiculous!

29

However sweetly, gently or charmingly you diminish someone, they will still feel unmistakably *diminished*.

30

We often assume that once a physical wound has healed, that is the end of it. We forget that the emotional wounds need to heal as well.

JULY

1

One way we oppress others is by denying them an opportunity to express their feelings towards us.

2

Take five minutes to look into the heart of a flower – and let your mind be still.

3

When you finally get around to criticising someone's behaviour, remember that although you've been aware of your feelings for months, or even years, they will come as a great surprise to the other person.

4

Feeling passionately puts colour into a grey world.

5

Let yourself off the hook – no one else can do it for you.

Next time you are planning a treat for someone you love, schedule in a treat for yourself as well.

7

The immense effort many of us put into controlling everything and everyone around us usually stems from a deep fear of rejection.

8

Physical symptoms of anxiety are worsened by denial: if you acknowledge the truth of what you feel, those symptoms will automatically subside.

9

Once a week, try a conscious choice to let go of your need to be right.

10

Try to acknowledge other people's feelings without judging them.

11

Other people's ups and downs often occur quite independently of our efforts to control their lives for them.

12

Always take the time to be clear about what *you* want before making any move towards tackling a situation.

13

Do you really want another drink or are you agreeing to avoid appearing unsociable?

14

Personal power comes from within ourselves – it is not dependent on outside approval or status.

15

The guilt you feel after saying no is only a measure of how difficult it was for you to do so.

16

Occasionally allow yourself a break from attending to others' needs – instead of waiting for others to give you their permission and blessing.

17

A good cry can be
a great release.

18

Aim high – if you come
in low, you can still praise
yourself highly.

19

Vulnerability should never be confused with weakness.

20

The quality of compassion can easily degenerate into pity and patronage.

21

Apportioning blame too readily temporarily eases the insecurity of living with uncertainty.

22

Our self-esteem is enhanced every time we face, acknowledge and survive any given anxiety.

23

If you find yourself complaining about always taking the 'helper' role, check whether or not you are being clear about your own needs.

24

We waste so much time and energy striving to be better than we are.

25

Enjoying your own orgasm in your own way retrieves it from being a rateable, standardised achievement and returns the experience to the realms of personal pleasure.

26

It is possible to acknowledge our dependence on others without losing our autonomy or self-respect.

27

Rudeness is never a necessary accompaniment to directness.

28

Don't allow others to invalidate your sense of humour just because you don't enjoy laughing at someone else's expense.

29

Responding with 'I don't mind' whenever you are asked to make a choice reinforces the habit of putting your responsibility in the hands of others.

30

Our sensitivity to criticism can cause us to misinterpret what we read or hear; take the time to check it out with the person concerned.

31

If your intuition tells you you cannot trust a person or situation, that is your reality and no amount of rationalising or wishful thinking will make it otherwise.

AUGUST

1

It helps to give vent, out loud, to all the unforgivable and awful things you've wanted to say to someone – while you're alone! Then you will be able to distinguish rubbish from reality.

2

Continuing to talk to someone while they are watching TV or on the phone gives a clear message that what you have to say is not important and not worth listening to.

3

You don't have to take a joke if you didn't ask for it.

4

The most likely way you'll get what you want is to ask for it directly and specifically.

5

It is essential, while remaining true to oneself, to acknowledge others' different and separate realities – otherwise we can get stuck in self-righteous delusion.

It is possible to be criticised and feel loved at the same time.

7

We reject real-life opportunities to be nurtured by waiting for a magical caretaker to materialise and meet all our fantasy requirements.

8

Trust your gut response – it is always a sign that you need to think twice about something before opening your mouth.

9

If you constantly dismiss yourself, you'll find others will dismiss you too.

10

Our sexuality doesn't cease to exist when others cease to see us as sexual objects.

11

When your reason for not being honest with someone is that the truth would be hurtful, remember that your own fear of rejection can also hold you back.

12

Instead of stopping at: 'You're great', or 'You're amazing', try making the extra effort to express specifically what you appreciate in someone.

13

Short-term compromises have the habit of becoming long-term prisons.

14

If someone says no to you, they are probably just saying no – not rejecting you outright.

15

It is possible to enjoy the havoc of your hormones if you can let go of your need to be in total control of everything.

16

As soon as you feel contempt for someone, you place yourself above them.

17

If you find you are sexually unaroused, this doesn't imply you are a sexual failure – more likely, the conditions you need to feel sexual arousal are not being met.

18

Try to find a few minutes every day to come back into you own skin and remember who *you* are, amid all your roles and responsibilities.

19

Our perceptions are distorted when our feelings run high.

When offering someone a criticism, keep to one item of behaviour only. That is all anyone can listen to or take in at any one time.

20

21

If you don't feel like smiling, don't smile.

22

We put so much emotional energy into finding and keeping the 'perfect relationship' that we often miss out on the more enduring joys of friendship.

23

Enjoy your emotions – those who criticise you for expressing them have usually lost touch with their own.

24

If you find yourself insisting that someone should follow your advice, you're probably bullying them.

25

You may not be able to have it all – but you can have it both ways!

26

It is low self-esteem which encourages us to suffer pain in silence rather than suffer possible disapproval.

27

People change at their own pace – we can't accelerate the process to suit our own needs.

28

Treasure those whose company prompts you to be playful and have fun – their gift to you is priceless.

29

As soon as you start worrying about the judgement of others, you cease being creative.

30

Learn to distinguish between straining and stretching yourself – the former leads to injury, the latter to development.

31

Even the role of the 'carer' can be addictive.

SEPTEMBER

1

Next time you catch sight of yourself in the mirror, blow yourself a little kiss – before the self-criticism starts!

2

It's easier to demand something from the standpoint of reproach than to ask openly and risk exposure and vulnerability.

3

Feeling sorry for someone has nothing to do with equality – it involves one person feeling kindly, benevolent and usually superior to another.

4

It is harder to confront a sexist or racist comment from someone we care for than from someone we are quite happy to dismiss.

5

It is a lifelong challenge, as women, to become subjects of our bodies when we have only experienced them as objects in the eyes of others.

When you offer someone a criticism, try and offer it as a gift rather than a punishment.

7

A deep inner emptiness is the abiding experience of most women – the biggest cream cake, the hottest sex, the most fulfilling occupation, the most adoring partner will do no more than assuage that emptiness for a while.

8

You can allow others to have feelings without taking on the responsibility for having caused them.

9

Blaming ourselves too readily protects us from the insecurity of accepting that life, by its very nature, is unpredictable and imperfect.

10

If you want help with a difficulty, remember that whining and whinging make most people go instantly deaf!

11

Our own self put-downs are often far more cruel than those we hear from other people.

12

Beat the hell out of a large cushion before trying to talk clearly to someone you're angry with.

13

Wanting to say no without ever feeling guilty is like wanting to climb a challenging mountain without ever feeling tired.

14

Don't expect support – just be open to it.

15

Seeking revenge is often understandable – but always aggressive.

16

If you sense deep down that you are shopping, drinking or eating to combat emptiness or depression, find the courage to ask yourself what you are feeling and then share this with someone you trust.

17

Even if you take a risk and make a mess of the situation, there is always something positive you can learn from the experience.

18

Emotions don't have to be either one thing or the other. They are usually a mixture of both.

19

Who are you when you are not attending to, thinking of, caring for others? *That* is the question.

20

Making a clear choice to put another's needs first is different from self-sacrifice on the altar of your own masochism.

21

Holding onto your own truth is a constant but necessary challenge in a world which encourages and rewards lies.

22

Next time you hear yourself saying, 'I don't mind', take a moment to check if you are being honest with yourself.

23

If you unexpectedly find yourself with time on your hands, instead of filling it by doing something useful, try passing the time just *being*.

We trade in the currency of guilt so automatically that we are hardly aware of it until we count our emotional pennies and seek to balance the accounts.

24

25

If you want your criticism to be heard, you will stand a better chance if you confine yourself to requesting one single, achievable change in the person's behaviour.

26

It is very hard to rid ourselves of the conviction that if only we could get it right, things would be different.

27

Manipulating someone 'for their own good' is a misappropriation of power – and such efforts are usually resisted.

28

You cannot feel sorry for yourself and skip at the same time.

29

Never confuse a self-put-down with real humility.

30

If you are depressed, tired or ill, it is madness to try to force yourself into a state of sexual arousal.

OCTOBER

1

Telling someone they've no right to be angry will only fuel the flames.

2

If you feel offended, say so – without causing offence in return.

3

Offer a compliment as a gift – freely given without regard to the other person's response.

4

Your feelings are simply your feelings – seeking someone to blame for causing them won't help them disappear.

5

When you preface your statement with: 'This may sound silly, but . . .', 'I know this isn't important, but . . .', 'Of course, I'm no expert, but . . .', you discourage listeners from taking you seriously.

Remember you can (and do) survive being told 'No' – and so can others.

7

Next time you find yourself gossiping about a friend, ask yourself if there is something you have avoided saying directly to them.

8

Have a temper tantrum occasionally – just don't try and communicate clearly at the same time.

9

It is worth building up a resource of particular activities, people or places which you know will restore you when you experience life's inevitable rejections.

10

Take time to concentrate on the process and pleasure of eating instead of hastily munching on the run.

11

Our need to be liked seduces us away from the path to real personal power.

12

Even if you're embarrassed or they're embarrassed, it is still worth saying thank you.

13

Self-esteem is buying something which fits comfortably and truthfully instead of squeezing into a smaller size and playing a self-punishing game of make-believe.

14

Refrain from phrases like 'I'm having a senior moment' when you get to a certain age; it compounds an already negative stereotype and lowers your self-esteem.

15

Each time we swallow back our emotions, we deny a vital part of our experience.

16

Being assertive does not mean always getting what you want: this could only be achieved by overriding others' feelings and needs along the way.

17

If someone is in tears, being with them silently and peacefully is often more helpful than rushing around for cups of tea or tissues.

18

If there's a stone in your shoe, you can remove it – or continue to walk, hoping the pain will eventually go away.

19

Next time you find yourself travelling on the merry-go-round of self-sacrifice, ask yourself, 'Is there really nothing I want in return . . . ever?'

20

It is quite a challenge to leave an argument with a clear statement of difference rather than insisting that one of you has to be right and the other wrong.

21

If you find yourself sinking into self-pity, take a moment to consider whether there are some different choices you could be making in your life.

22

You *can* probably please everybody all of the time – but is it really worth the cost?

23

Don't wait until the next time before you say something – making the time to confront a situation before it recurs increases your chances of handling it effectively.

24

The power that will be released when women stop punishing themselves will be an enormous force for change in the world.

25

Practise walking lightly through heavy situations.

26

Far from being grounds for criticism, the quality of oversensitivity should be celebrated as a beacon in an emotionally unenlightened world.

27

Blaming others is the easiest way to divert ourselves from taking responsibility for our own feelings and behaviour.

28

Excessive criticism will severely damage anyone's sense of self-worth.

29

The role of 'carer' wraps us like a familiar warm coat – we are afraid that, without it, we might freeze to death.

30

Whether making love or a fruit cake, try focusing on the pleasure of the process rather than worrying about the quality of the end product.

31

Even if you keep her well-hidden most of the time, allow the witch in you some clear means of expression every now and then.

NOVEMBER

1

What are you really waiting for?

2

Acting a little crazily (in the eyes of others) is often the best way to retain your sanity.

3

Don't confuse blaming and punishing yourself with genuinely taking responsibility for your behaviour.

4

Other people's feelings do not necessarily have anything to do with your behaviour.

5

Gossip can be like a drug
– easily available, slightly
taboo, temporarily enjoyable,
but ultimately poisonous
to the entire system.

The energy wasted in worrying
whether someone is hurt
or angry or disappointed,
could be saved by a simple,
clear, direct enquiry.

7

There is no
single right way.

8

Contrary to popular belief,
anger can be a highly
constructive emotion.

9

Never be ashamed to be 'heart-full' – even if you're in heartless surroundings.

10

Rejection can be survived, and we can be stronger as a result of the experience.

11

Failing to confront unfair criticism is an effective way of putting yourself down.

12

Saying no to someone one cares for is, for most women, as natural as cutting off one's arm.

13

A hairline crack in a relationship easily grows into an unbridgeable chasm.

14

Know when to remove yourself silently from a situation in which you feel uneasy.

15

When someone knows clearly and specifically what you would like to be different, they find it easier to hear and accept what is currently unsatisfactory.

16

Learn how to state clearly that you disagree without getting into a battle of who is right and who is wrong.

17

There are many erotic pleasures to be enjoyed in everyday life, if we don't confuse them with sexual activity.

18

Next time you're swamped with guilt, ask yourself what you're angry about.

19

Authority becomes oppression when we don't allow others to express their responses to our actions and decisions.

20

Exercising your right to choose may well incur reproach, because being reminded of one's own ability to choose is often an uncomfortable experience.

21

Instead of politely waiting to interrupt someone who is abusing you over the phone, you can hang up.

22

Don't deny anxiety: learn how to breathe into and through it to find your clarity on the other side.

23

Giving up the need to be seen to be right allows for a lot more flexibility in life.

24

Don't wait until someone is leaving or dying before you tell them how much you value them.

25

When your heart melts, don't be afraid to let it show.

26

Often we feel empowered to criticise someone only when we feel the authority of being *right* – but criticism given from this superior standpoint will always be met with a defensive response.

27

Clear anger is a vital though unfamiliar aspect of love.

28

Singing – or simply allowing your voice to make large sounds – is a wonderful release of tension.

29

However much you think you are cloaking your aggression, it will always be picked up on and responded to in kind.

30

The best way to stop feeling threatened by someone expressing their anger is to become more familiar and comfortable with this emotion in yourself.

DECEMBER

1

The intention to set aside 30 minutes a day for oneself is easy. Achieving this aim, for most of us, is the equivalent of climbing an emotional Everest.

2

Laugh when you want to laugh – not just to be one of the crowd.

3

There is nothing so personally empowering as making a clear choice.

4

Sometimes it is wiser to keep quiet.

5

It is more honest to use the word 'angry' to describe your feelings when this is appropriate, rather than settling for 'upset' or 'hurt'.

Never attempt to offer a criticism of your lover when you are in bed together. Make a time to talk when you are both less naked.

7

Focus on *one* thing you would like to be different in any given situation – this is the first vital step out of the mire of helplessness.

8

Are you only holding back because you can't guarantee getting it right?

9

Rubbing someone's face in their own inadequacies offers us temporary relief from punishing the weak and imperfect aspects of ourselves.

10

If you exercise your right to change your mind, remember the accompanying responsibility – to communicate your decision as soon as possible.

11

Never embark on a mission to communicate a request if you haven't first decided what it is you want.

12

Listen to and trust what your heart tells you.

13

Don't sabotage yourself by tackling a situation that is too difficult to handle – this only leads to loss of confidence and despair.

14

The torment of punishing ourselves for not getting it right is often preferable to experiencing the helplessness of piloting through chaos.

15

When dealing with money, we often allow ourselves to be manipulated by our own fears and a low sense of self-worth.

16

Starting from a place of self-acceptance enables us to be intimate without swamping others or being swamped ourselves.

17

If you feel manipulated by another's question or statement, encourage them to express their feelings or wishes *directly* to you.

18

Our self-esteem is strengthened when we stop imposing grandiose and impossible expectations on ourselves.

19

Fear of looking foolish prevents us criticising someone directly because, in doing so, we risk finding out that our perceptions are wrong.

20

Through clearly expressing our anger, we are able to touch the edge of our joy.

21

We tend to overestimate the number of people who are truly dependent on us for their survival.

22

The greater the loss of your self-esteem, the more you depend on others' approval to compensate that loss.

23

It is the *being* of sexuality which we have lost through our obsession with the *doing*.

24

If someone criticises you unjustly, it is important to express your disagreement but also invite the other person to clarify what has prompted the criticism.

25

A simple, heartfelt, appreciative comment is the best gift of all.

26

It is easier to package a request using reproach and guilt as leverage than risk being told no.

27

Treat yourself with gentleness and kindness. It may sound simple, but is often the hardest thing to do.

28

Personal power is being true to yourself – it has nothing to do with winning or losing.

29

Don't confine sexuality to the genitals – sexual energy spreads throughout our bodies and throughout our lives.

30

We spend so much time anticipating and reacting to others that it is easy to lose sight of our own feelings and needs.

31

Whatever you choose to give, make sure it is duty free.

PAGES OF YOUR OWN

From time to time, we hear or read someone's words which strike a chord. Whether they're wise, witty, serious or profound, they linger in our minds and hearts. The following blank pages provide an opportunity to personalise this book with thoughts and sayings that have particular meaning for you.

PAGES OF YOUR OWN

PAGES OF YOUR OWN

PAGES OF YOUR OWN

PAGES OF YOUR OWN

PAGES OF YOUR OWN